PHANTOMS

poems by

Joanna Grisham

Finishing Line Press
Georgetown, Kentucky

PHANTOMS

ACKNOWLEDGMENTS

Thank you to the editors of *The Emerson Review* for publishing the poem
"Phantoms" and *Gleam*, who published "Near Totality."

I want to extend my deepest gratitude to everyone who has read these poems
and offered critiques and ideas, including Charles Booth, Mitzi Cross,
Malcolm Glass, and Barry Kitterman, who have read most of my work in
recent years and who continue to offer me encouragement and support.
Thank you to Amy Wright, who read many of these poems early on, gave me
invaluable feedback, and urged me to write the Georgia Sanitarium series.
Stephanie Dugger, thank you for your keen eyes and your lasting friendship.
Thanks to my family for giving me much to write about and for loving me
still, even when I write about hard things. And, lastly, thank you to my
daughter, Lennon, for her patience with me while I was working on this
book, mostly during her summer break, and, of course, to my wife, my best
friend, my biggest supporter, Jenny, who has my heart, always.

Publisher: Leah Huete de Maines
Editor: Christen Kincaid
Cover Art: Cricket Press design 'Wood Wraith'
Author Photo: Danielle Logan and Gracie Carver
Cover Design: Elizabeth Maines McCleavy

Order online: www.finishinglinepress.com
also available on amazon.com

Author inquiries and mail orders:
Finishing Line Press
PO Box 1626
Georgetown, Kentucky 40324
USA

Table of Contents

For all the ghosts out there,
dead or otherwise,
and for Jenny, always

PHANTOMS

For Jenny and Carol

Your mother scratches the air below her thigh,
the nothing-place where her leg should
be. *I can still feel it,* she says, embarrassed,
pulling the white sheet to her chest
like a child facing a midnight-monster.
You smooth her hair, say she's beautiful
and strong, picture her dancing in the kitchen,
making Halloween sounds into a spoon,
while you balance on a chair, hair combed
into a vampire-point, plastic teeth
cutting your gums. Suddenly, you remember
her tan calves, smooth and muscular
from standing all day at the video
store and *The Brave Little Toaster*
poster she brought home for you, *Baywatch*
for your brother. You recall, too, the sugar
you spooned into her mouth, trips
to the ER instead of Friday night parties,
the day your father left and she wouldn't
open the bathroom door, the sound of
her voice after she learned to talk again,
the way she wore her hair before and
after, the two lives you lived with her—
everything that led to this moment, this
loss, this beginning of an end. She
looks out the window, turns to face you,
the sun's rays streak the hospital tile, her brown
eyes are dark, innocent, full of disbelief.
I'm sorry, she says, when she reaches again
for the blank space, a memory her body
cannot purge, *it was just right there.*

They knew she could not talk,
would not say a word when they drove
her up to the asylum, the place of her
eventual death. Her papers said, *Unmarried*
and *18*. Her papers said, *patient is dumb*
but can hear. Her papers said she was born
that way. She would not feed

herself, would not pull the gown
over her head. *Idit*, they wrote, misspelling
the word, and led her to the windowed room,
where she watched the sun shine
on the garden below. They wrote in her chart,
violent and *destructive*. Her papers
said the baby was born dead seven months

before. But no one asked Dora,
girl without a voice, girl with a child's
mind, about the baby. No one asked Dora
who had held her down, no need to cover
her mouth with a dirty hand or pillow.
Her papers said, she was *weeke minded*
from Birth. The baby must have kicked

her from the inside, must have
fluttered and swam sometimes, might
have made her sick or dizzy. No one asked
Dora if she had held her baby before they
took it away, buried it beneath the pines
with her other kin, a graveside she would
never visit. A name she could never speak.

GHOSTS

I.

A shadow bends across the hall,
makes itself tall and pointed on the
knotty pine wall beside my bed where
I watch it with angled eyes, my
breath sharp as the glass shard he
pulled from my knee after he punched
the window. He longs to be kind,
but her ghost will not stop whispering
lies, telling him love is a small,
weak thing, meant to make him soft.

II.

Hungry dogs wag their tongues and bounce
themselves over piles of trash to greet
him twice a week at the city dump,
where they pounce and clamor toward the
water bowl he fills for them, his hands
rough and black from sanding and polishing,
as he scavenges for new treasures—an
antique dresser, a broken desk,
some rusty caster wheels, and, once
a Casper the Friendly Ghost
doll for me. Mama washes it three times,
but it still looks grey, faded, unclean.

III.

He picks me up from daycare, stops
at the gas station outside town
where they sell me his Miller Lite and
Vantage smokes. On the way home,
I drink chocolate milk from a brown
paper sack and balance my candy
cigarette between my fingers. He
asks if I had a good day and turns
up the radio before I can

answer. We coast down the country
road in the long, white car he calls Ghost.

IV.
I watch him pray in the shadows
of the den, kneeling amid a
glittering sunset that lights him up,
a golden Lucifer,
angry and wanting, falling from the
heavens, hands outstretched, sometimes,
or folded under his chin, as he whispers,
I'm sorry. Later, in a black out,
he tells his mother's ghost she's the
reason he cannot love; she's the one
sitting on his chest, dream-demon,
haunting him, stealing his breath.

V.
Every night I dream of our house,
the one that burned down. My upstairs
room painted black. I sit
cross-legged, a little girl
among piles of trash, witch's hat
covering my tangled hair. He
stands in the doorway, and I know
I should invite him in, but he's
not really there, so I ignore
him, continue to sort and stack.
I'll see his ghost again tomorrow,
in the black room in the burnt house
in some other past I can almost
taste—chocolate, ash, sugar,
vodka, metal, wood, fire.

WINTER

For Jenny

Remember that blue and white
winter we spent in bed, wrapped
in blankets, longing for more
snow days to make us forget
our classes, our jobs at the mall?
We wandered by the river,
white-cold and speckled with starlight,
feigned freezing so we could hold hands.

…I want you to remember me
kissing you in the back
of a bar, pulling you into
a smoky hallway, my hand on
your mouth. At home, I'd tug
your shirt over your head, toss
it into a heap of laundry
I never seemed to get around to.
We'd lie in bed, watching the moon
hang outside the window,
waiting for sunrise, and fall asleep
tangled in sheets, as if we'd
been trapped, the prey of some
larger thing we hadn't yet faced.
(And it would come for us.)
Then, we'd laugh at how perfect
it was to fall into forever
with your best friend. We didn't
know how easy it might be to
lose that person, to lose yourself.

It's six a.m., winter light comes
in around the blackout
curtains, bright little fingers
to yank us into a new day.
A sound machine plays ocean
waves on repeat. The electronic
sea is maddening. *Crash, crash.*
We've followed the books to a T,
recreated the womb, and now
our baby sleeps in my arms
because she will not sleep any
other way. You breathe deeply
beside me, your eyelids flutter,
a dream maybe. Of me, maybe?
Of *then?* I know I could touch you
if I just reached across the pillow.

BUTTERCUPS

After he died, I dreamed a cabin in the woods, a place
we'd never been with paneled walls and plaid curtains.
Dinner table dappled with sunlight, pink and yellow
and white, like those sunsets by the pond so long ago,
when I was a little girl, and he was too drunk to notice

me watching. The table was set, bowls of green beans,
mashed potatoes, an apple pie so fragrant I could smell
the cinnamon and butter. I walked to the window,
smiling at the day's beauty, the quaintness of it all.
He stood on the hillside, not so far away, shielding his

eyes from the sun, younger than he'd been when he died,
curls blowing, (Where was his hat?), mustache trimmed neat
like he wore it at the beach, when he was healthy, resigned
to live in this world. And like those memories, everything
was golden, the trees, the grass, my father, as if viewed

through a sunlit filter. *Come inside, Daddy. Dinner's
ready,* I called. He turned, held my gaze, shook his head,
said, *You know I can't do that, kid. I can't ever come back
inside.* I reached through the window to pull him close. *But
everything you love is right here,* I said, wanting

to believe that had always been true, knowing it never
was. He tapped his chest, *Everything I love is right here
now. Go on without me.* I watched him fade into the
shining sky. There were buttercups growing where
he'd stood, bright yellow, always come too soon.

EVERY CLOUD...

Before she left me for good, she was late
coming home from church one Friday night.
She arrived with a scribbled list, reasons
we had to call it quits. I knew what was
coming that weekend. Still, I waited
on her back porch, smoking too many
cigarettes, sipping wine, hoping she'd make
it fast this time, so I could join my friends
downtown, celebrating uncertainty
with the licking of wrists, the thumping
of too-loud bass. She had notes on a sermon
about grace and forgiveness, reminded
me about the shiny linings living
behind the clouds. And I nodded, pretended
to believe her, touched her arm as she read
from the Word, whispered-wet into her ear,
until she forgot the list, at least
for a little while. Then, I cried, so she'd
fuck me one last time before I left her
kneeling beside the bed, rocking back
and forth in prayer, lost in a whir I had
to needle through on my way to the bathroom.
She begged me to stay and repent, but we both
knew I wasn't sorry for the right parts.

SHE REMEMBERS
For my sister, Les

She remembers NYC's wet glitter streets,
blinking billboards, belligerent horns, vendors
laughing with their heads thrown back, bars packed
with people in black t-shirts, pink cocktails
in hand, smoke-Os floating above their heads.
She remembers the perfect pizza she inhaled
at midnight on the subway, even though
she was supposed to drop three pounds, and
the way her agent pronounced her name
with a snaky sssss in the middle and how
she felt when she slipped on the fur coat, gave
herself a hug, spinning around the room,
cameras flashing, the pointy featured women
from hair and makeup pulling and smoothing
and shaping her into someone she'd dreamt
of becoming since she was a child sitting
at her grandmother's feet, sewing together
scraps to make a little dress for her doll,
something glamorous and sparkling like her
secret fantasies. She remembers the phone
ringing in her room every night, her mother
calling from Tennessee where her father
was still drunk and her brother was still gone
and her baby sister was still sleeping
in the t-shirt she'd left behind, spritzed with her
favorite perfume, and how her voice caught
in her throat when she told her agent she had
to go and the way the city looked, sharp and gray
and metallic from the plane, like some outer
space dream she must have had, her sister's
arms around her waist when she dropped her suitcase
by the door and the way her mother didn't look
up from the kitchen stove. Now in her fifties,
tired, single, again, she stands naked in the bathroom,
considers the green eyes in the mirror
and recalls how she felt pretty and wanted
and alive years ago, before she returned,

married and divorced and married and divorced,
before the kids came—kids she loves, of course.
Like Plath's figs, she could choose but one piece
of fruit before it fell rotten to the earth. (But how
do we know when we've tasted the sweetest
bite?) She grabs her keys, heads to work and
remembers her other self, that other life, that faraway
place, still there, alive, shining and loud.
Sometimes, she can almost taste the pizza.

KIDS

The smack of high fives echoes
down the hall, eight-year-olds sit
crisscross-applesauce with
check-yes-or-no-notes crumpled
in classroom corners and half-folded
spelling tests poking out of backpack
pockets, sticker-slapped with *Wow!*
Great! Super Job! bound
for refrigerator doors
in some homes, like mine, where tired,
proud mothers fry chicken and
bake biscuits and give away
hugs just for entering a room.

But he never gets any
stickers or do-you-like-me notes,
or high fives from the other boys,
and I don't know about the hugs
or warm biscuits. He's in time-out
again. I watch him from my desk.
He stands, arms folded, brow furrowed,
glaring into the coat-closet,
his hands two balled up fists, clenching
and unclenching. Alcohol
on his mother's breath when she
picks him up at three, dead daddy
in a city he's never
seen, Jesus on the mainline.
The song says, "tell Him what you want,"
but how are we supposed to know?

MARY—GEORGIA SANITARIUM, SUMMER 1911

She dances in the hallway, mumbles prayers,
Geechee incantations for her dead siblings,

the ones she has seen glowing in bedroom
corners since she was six. And now, with them,

her own nine babies who did not survive,
cherubs floating in and out of shadow,

smiling and pointing, demanding her ear.
She quivers, shouts, annoys the doctors

with her ability to remain *exalted on the ward,*
because how dare she feel any joy. She was

at home praying when they took her, probably
speaking in tongues, ringing her hands

as she danced circles around the kitchen.
Hallucinations, they said, but she knows

the faces of her dead when they reveal
themselves at dawn, shiny visitors sent to carry

her through another day. She knows the voice
of her god, how it warms her throat as she lifts

her arms, shakes her head, shuffles her feet,
how it comforts her. She tells the doctors,

That's not strange about hearing a dead person's
voice. A lot of people die and then come back and talk.

MY FATHER WANTED TO BE AN ACTOR

he tells me, as we sit on a borrowed
balcony by the beach, the sea singing
below, the moon shining on the sand.

What? I say, surprised, *But you hate
attention.* He laughs, *I know. I'm
just saying that's what I wanted to be.*

I close my eyes, listen to the lilted
voices of children with flashlights
looking for sand crabs, hear them squeal

when they spot the skeletal bodies
scurrying over the white dunes. *What
kind of roles would you want to play?* I ask,

picturing him as an outlaw on the edge
of some kind of violence, or a
wiry gangster hauling in snitches

to face a greasy boss, who sits
behind a long table dusted with
cocaine and littered with bottles

of booze. My father has been sober
three years now. I carry his
other self in my heart, though

I try to forget. I cannot
imagine him a good guy in these
fictions flashing in my mind. He leans

back in his chair, rubs the scruff of hair
around his smoky mouth. *Maybe someone
like Gable or Newman,* he says, shrugging.

A leading man? I ask. *Villains have
more fun on screen.* He shakes
his head, clicks his lighter, the flame

flickers in the dark across from me.
Not in real life though, he says. I pull
my jacket around my shoulders, toss

him a blanket. He's frail now, dying, but we
don't know it yet. He'll be gone in seven months,
cancer. The TV plays in the condo. He watches

it through the glass door. *I can't believe
I never knew this about you,* I say, but there
are so many things I don't know, will

never know. He rubs his bony knees through
the blanket. *I always felt so ugly,* he says,
finally, and I want to take his hand, tell

him how wonderful he is…now. *Daddy, don't
say that.* He smiles. *I just wanted to be
beautiful,* he says, almost whispering. I look

away, find the moon, a distant star, then
see a child of light on the beach. *We all do,*
I say, watching the girl scoop up her treasure.

HOLY GHOST REVIVAL

A prophet has come to foretell of miracles
and tragedies. He smears our heads with oil,
beckons us to move forward and be filled or
perish. It's a Holy Ghost revival.
An elderly woman abandons her
walker to dance across the stage, head thrown
back in ecstasy, laughing like the mad.
Delighted and reckless, she knocks the hymnals
to the floor, falls into the piano
player who continues to bang on
the keys—a cacophony of sound
punctuates the collision. The chorus
continues, *You can have it, if you want it.*
A man shouts, *Hallelujah,* leaps over
pews, righteous track star in a rumpled suit,
jumping for Jesus. He has forgotten
the day, unfinished paperwork piled on
his desk, forms to sign and send. Now, he is
lost in the God-space. He is found in sublime
chaos. Some of the kids fake it, jump and
strut, stagger into each other hoping
to graze a breast, sniff the hair of their crush.
But I fall to my knees and mean it—I long
to be transformed. There are hands on my
body, voices on all sides. I'm lifted
to my feet, my chin, my cheeks, my mouth
smacked loose. In a corner, women huddle,
stammer, and sway, while God gives coded clues
that only the gifted can decipher,
and I worry He'll tell them my secret,
betray my trust because I'm not holy
enough, not worthy of saving, and that may
be true, but still I pray until my mouth
breaks open and my tongue unleashes tones
I cannot comprehend, and I know, then, why
they want it: it feels so good to be gone.

MY MOTHER'S HANDS
For my mother, Debbie

My legs dangle from the counter. I scoop flour into my mother's hands—
black coffee, fried eggs, sticky ball of dough in my mother's hands.

Mouths open like eager fish—*Amen Amen*—preacher shouts
of golden streets and new bodies, but will I know my mother's hands?

A photo: white sheet cake, my name in careful green icing, new
doll in my lap, three candles to blow out, shadow of my mother's hands.

At the foot-washing service we sing songs of sacrifice and blood;
I watch my sister's feet sink to the bottom of the basin below my mother's
    hands.

I dream of waves and sand, a beach dotted with pirate's gold. A storm
brews at sea—we hide in the lee of a rock. I hold tight to my mother's
    hands.

She named me Joanna, God's gracious gift, but what do I know of grace?
Broken sleep, leaking breasts. I long to be held by my mother's hands.

NEIGHBORS

We watched from the upstairs window,
rain pearling on the black body bag,
bejeweled and bulging from burden,
our sliding door foggy from midday
heat. We didn't know him, but we cried.
He lived alone, downstairs. I said hello
to him once at the mailboxes, annoyed
that he took up so much space, forced
to touch him when I squeezed by. And
another time, while we drank Moscow
Mules on our balcony and admired
our container garden, bell peppers
streaked purple and green like the tie-dyed
shirts we wore as kids, we saw him lurch
out of a taxi, gripping a brown
paper sack, oxygen tank in tow.
He wore a hospital gown, grey joggers,
sweaty and stained. I shook my head, popped
a tomato into my mouth,
pretended not to notice when he strained
to heave the tank onto the sidewalk.
That was months before the guy below
us, the Greek guy who always sounded
like he was yelling, called the landlord
to complain about the smell, months
before we heard the sound one Sunday
night, rhythmic and hollow, like earthquakes
juddering our unit awake.
For over an hour, we listened
and then walked around the building,
hand in hand, two lost children, still
scared of the dark, using our phones
as flashlights. Outside we heard
muffled voices, crying babies,

too-loud TVs. Later, we felt the floor
vibrate again and again, reminding
us we were not alone in that world.
They finally found the body,
had to saw through the security
chain on the door. *It was him,* you said,
sounding faraway, eyes fixed on the
flashing lights outside, *The sound.* And
I knew you were right. *But we looked,*
I said. *We tried.* I drew a square
on the window, framing the scene,
a picture we'd never forget.
We don't know how he died, just that he
lived alone, and it was days before
anyone found him, and we never asked
his name, or the name of the Greek man,
or the name of the new girl
who moved into the dead guy's
apartment two weeks later, after
the deep clean. We wondered if anyone
told her. Probably not. Who is she
anyway? Just some neighbor.

SHIFT

At the park, I walk to the
river and watch you swing—push
into the wind, toward something
new, just beyond. Your mane
of curls wild in the breeze.
I stand behind you, in the
shadows of trees that pattern
themselves black against the
pale-blue sky, marionettes
dangling from the clouds. You say,
I spidered a girl on this swing, once.

And I suddenly
remember church camp, twelve-years-old,
red dress hiked up around
my hips, my body pressed against
some older boy, our legs dangling
like a spider, my panties
bumping against him with every
push-kick. There, on the swings
with a dozen other kids
who already forgot
the worship service just
forty minutes earlier.
The counselors made us
repent. And I was full of
sorrow that night. But, days later,
when I asked Missy to spider
with me, I felt something change,
shift, as I pushed harder and
harder into the night air.
She giggled in my ear, hid
her face in my neck. And we
were not sorry. (Where is she now?)

I'm still thinking of church
camp and Missy and her
sunflower hair when I
commit you to memory.
Long after I forget
your eyes, your voice, I'll
remember the day you brought
me to your hometown, showed me
where you once lived, rode a bike,
dreamed of escape. You could have
been her, and I would have lost you.

WHAT I KNOW

I learn many lessons by the light of the TV,
the blinking blue-black world all shadow and glow.
Nothing is real. What I feel doesn't change what I see.

I've left it on all night for years to keep me company,
a strobe-light of faces flashing, show after show.
I learn many lessons by the light of the TV,

erase a morning of Sunday school rants with movies
about outer space, try to ease the woe.
Nothing is real. What I feel doesn't change what I see,

but sitcoms make me forget the screaming misery,
laugh track to drown out raised voices below.
I learn many lessons by the light of the TV.

Preacher says God forgives all, but His love is not free.
I flip through the channels and know what I know.
Nothing is real. What I feel doesn't change what I see.

My father lies dying on a couch right in front of me,
while a televangelist speaks in tongues, murmuring low.
I learn many lessons by the light of the TV.
Nothing is real. What I feel doesn't change what I've seen.

FIRST CRUSH

When I dream of her, she's all loops
          and ooos on my lips, tart

like communion wine, sweet
          like Dreamsicles.

I trace our initials in the dirt,
          cross them out before she sees,

carve tree-trunk declarations
          at the far edge of the playground,

pray she'll say hi to me in the hall,
          cry in the bathroom when

she's absent, let her use my pencil
          sharpener, the one with the pink

Troll Doll hair, hold my breath
          when she tells me she like-likes

someone from class. It's not me,
          of course, but when the moon

shines through my window later,
          I'll imagine she's there, floating

above me, reaching into my chest,
          tearing out chapter one, and flipping

to the part where she kisses my silver
          star-shaped mouth.

AFTERLIFE

Perhaps, he still runs wild among the trees,
somehow a child, his ghost soaring beneath
a dome of fog and clouds. He has found bees
to trap and love, hides them under a sheath,

opaque, heavy like her kindness. He once
held her close when she was sick with fever,
hands shook, breath stopped, as he reached out to touch
her brow with a damp cloth. The clock never

ticked so loudly. Oh! to be here and there.
Time is a lie we tell ourselves so we
can shape our lives into something to bear.
Preacher says more will come, so much to see.

But she is not with him. He flies alone,
golden honey drips warm, sweet on his tongue.

LAMENTATION
For my father, Max

We scattered along the beach that night,
the gulf slapping at our ankles, seven of us,
each holding a cup of your ashes, gray
as the sand beneath our feet, tiny fragments
of bone, sharp as seashells, pieces of you
to hold, to give back to the earth, to the sea
you feared and loved. I gripped the red cup,
knelt by the water. The moon hid behind
a cloud. I was thankful for the darkness,
worried we'd get in trouble—a perfect
goodbye for you—man at odds with the law,
always vowing to speak softer, drink less, love more.

I hesitated, standing at the water's
edge, remembering our last trip, how
you sobbed when you saw the ocean after
decades. *Bring me back when I'm gone, kid.*
I thought it would be years, not months. All
around me, couples strolled by holding hands,
children toted buckets and flashlights,
oblivious. My free hand rested on my belly,
where a new life kicked and swam. I thought
of the well-meaning person who told me
you might be an angel now, said you picked
my baby just for me, sent her to Earth.
How absurd, I thought, shaking
my head, remembering all the times you carried
me out of church, a crying toddler, held
my hand under the trees outside, taught me
to pull the honeysuckle strings and lick the sweetness.

My hands shook as I crouched on the shore,
tilted the cup into the waves, let the water
carry you away from me, little by little, into
darkness, the unknown. *I love it because it's endless,*
you said, months earlier, staring into the shimmering

ocean as if you could somehow see its end if you
looked long enough. My baby flipped
and danced, as I rinsed the rest of you from my cup,
making sure there was none left in the bottom.

JOEY—CENTRAL STATE HOSPITAL, FORMERLY KNOWN AS THE GEORGIA SANITARIUM, SUMMER 2010

Sticky heat smothers us silent
as scolded children. We ignore
the KEEP OUT sign and tiptoe
across a lawn of broken limbs

and tall grass near THE MOST
HAUNTED BUILDING
ON CAMPUS! according to
local lore. I don't believe

in ghosts, not the dead kind, but
our escort, a supernatural
devotee, eagerly pushes
open a door—how is it possibly

unlocked?—and boldly ducks
inside. Jenny yells, *Wait,* but
I follow our friend into the
vacant building once inhabited

by the state's MOST SINISTER
MENTAL HEALTH PATIENTS—
mothers, daughters, sisters,
servants—women who could not

be tamed or comprehended by
the men who wished to shut them
up, lock them away. Women
suffering from post-partum

depression after having a baby
every year for twelve years, only
to see two survive, women who heard
the voice of God while hanging

blankets on the line to dry, women
whipped by abusive husbands, beaten
by impatient brothers. I'm shocked
breathless when I step through

the doorway. The floor is littered
with Coke bottles and Doritos bags,
maybe from unhomed citizens who
fear another night on the street more

than the pissed off spirits of dead
women. The sudden blast of arctic
air makes no sense, so I retreat
to the Georgia heat, where my future

wife bites her nails on the sidewalk
down the hill. *Why did you go in there?*
she asks, taking my hand. I say
I only wanted to know what it felt like.

Our friend climbs out a window.
The door wouldn't open when I tried to get out,
she yells, smiling, exhilarated. *That place
is totally haunted.* Jenny looks at me. I look

away, thinking of nightfall and the people
who willingly climb inside, again
and again, seeking shelter,
munching chips, huddling together

when the security guard makes
his rounds, and I think of the women
held against their will, strapped
to beds and chairs, injected with drugs,

shocked bright, only to go dull,
again, and I am thankful
I am here.
Now.

NEAR TOTALITY

1.
Late afternoon sun sends streaks of light across
the floor. Particles of dancing-dust hover and twirl around
the room like glowing fairies. I plunge my hands into too-hot
dishwater, careful of the menacing knives, and watch my
toddler scribble in a notepad at her little round table
in the corner. She hums, smiles at her work, obviously
pleased with the chaotic nests on the page, joyous eruptions.
She stops to watch the yellow leaves fall outside the
kitchen window, waves her hands to say goodbye.

2.
I often think of my brother's face the day he wrecked
his dirt bike in the woods near our house. How he climbed
the hill, pushing the bike alongside him, his cheeks streaked
with syrupy blood, how he told me to *shut up* when I asked
what happened from the patch of dirt where I rolled cars
down a mound, how he cried when our mother cleaned his
wounds, tears slicing through the mud and blood, making
zigzag roads across his face, a map to some secret city,
a faraway place he'll spend his whole life searching for.

3.
The graveyard slants and dips along the hill beside an old
Baptist church, where we tiptoe around chipped headstones
and faded silk flowers in search of dirt for spells we will never
cast. We aren't witches, though the moonlight makes us feel
powerful, bold enough to hold hands as we giggle like children,
scooping dirt into a plastic bottle we find in the trunk of your car.
We joke about the people we'll curse, the old lovers we'll ruin.
Sixteen years later, you're my wife, and I keep that bottle
of dirt tucked away in a box in the top of our closet, just in case.

4.

My father wants to go night fishing, so I meet him near
the river, where he climbs into my pickup truck and points
me toward his spot. We crouch on a muddy bank, catching
crappie. He talks about the water level and erosion and how
hot it has been all summer, worries about the fish and
the forest. I worry about him, puffing on his inhaler,
lighting up a cigarette. *We ought to fry these up soon,* he
says, and I say, *sure.* I find the fish years later, waiting
in the back of his deep freeze on the afternoon of his funeral.

5.

The blood moon rises above the bald cypress trees, standing
guard like ancient gods along the shore. I watch her reflection
ripple and shine, a glittering skeleton stretched across the lake,
extending her long arm as if to pull me in. A few hours from now,
I'll be forty, and the moon will slide into Earth's shadow, hide her
silver face, while I stand, arms stretched above my head, eyes
open and clear, listening to the water lick and lap with shiny white
tongues as if the shore were something to devour. I'll remember
how the sign said the forest is underwater now, but it's still there.

Notes

The poems "DORA—GEORGIA SANITARIUM, SUMMER 1910"[1] and "MARY—GEORGIA SANITARIUM, SUMMER 1911"[2] are based on the experiences of actual patients whose stories are analyzed and preserved in Mab Segrest's 2020 book titled *Administrations of Lunacy: Racism and the Haunting of American Psychiatry at The Milledgeville Asylum.* The italicized words in both poems are taken from the patients' charts, which Segrest includes in her book. Below, I have provided footnotes for the patients' medical records referenced in Segrest's book.

I saw Segrest speak when she was the Newell Visiting Scholar at Georgia College & State University. Her lecture inspired another poem in this collection called: "JOEY—CENTRAL STATE HOSPITAL, FORMERLY KNOWN AS THE GEORGIA SANITARIUM, SUMMER 2010."

[1]"Dora Williams" (pseudonym), Central State Hospital Medical Case Records, Feb. 1909-Nov. 1926, Public Health Central State Hospital, RG-SG-26-12-048, Vol. 2193, April to Aug.1912, 135.

[2]"Mary Roberts" (pseudonym), Central State Hospital Medical Case Records, Feb. 1909-Nov. 1926, Public Health Central State Hospital, RG-SG-S 26-12-048, Vol. 1-2193, April 1909-Aug. 1912, Georgia Archives.

Joanna Grisham grew up in a small town in middle Tennessee where she spent a lot of time playing with her imaginary friends. As a child, she daydreamed about becoming an international spy, a paleontologist, or a soap opera villain. In college, she took an intro to creative writing class and fell in love with words and the worlds they could create. She went on to earn an MFA in Creative Writing from Georgia College & State University, leading her down the path of teaching and writing. She was named a finalist for the 2021-2022 Very Short Fiction Contest at the Tennessee Williams & New Orleans Literary Festival and a finalist for the 2021 Ember Chasm Review Flash Fiction Contest. Her work has appeared in *Gleam, The Emerson Review, The Write Launch, On the Run,* and other places.